DARLING, QUIT APOLOGIZING:

THAT IS SO LAST SEASON.

TAYLOR N. TAYLOR

DISCLAIMER.

Copyright by Taylor N. Taylor, 2022. All rights reserved.
This document should not be duplicated or reproduced in any form without the express permission of the author.

TABLE OF CONTENTS

DARLING, QUIT APOLOGIZING: THAT IS SO LAST SEASON.

DISCLAIMER.

TABLE OF CONTENTS

INTRODUCTION.

CHAPTER 1: EXCUSES TO DROP
    EXCUSE 1: I'M NOT A GOAL-ORIENTED PERSON
    EXCUSE 2: I DON'T HAVE TIME.
    EXCUSE 3: IT'S ALREADY BEEN DONE.

CHAPTER 2: ATTITUDES TO ADOPT
    STOP ASKING PERMISSION
    TAKE CREDIT FOR YOUR WORK
    ASK FOR HELP

CHAPTER 3: SKILLS TO ACQUIRE
    PLANNING
    CONFIDENCE
    PERSISTENCE
    LEAD-(H)ER-SHIP

CONCLUSION

DARLING, BELIEVE IN YOUR DANG SELF!

INTRODUCTION.

There are numerous reasons (and excuses) for why women give up on their dreams.

Think of the world that would result if every woman pursued what she really wanted without worrying about getting judged or being plagued by self-doubts.

It is very likely that it would be an entirely different and altogether better world if just 3 percent of the women on earth would fearlessly follow their dreams.

Unfortunately, the fact remains that a saddening great number of women are neglecting what they want – and there are reasons for this.

First of all, it's in our nature to seek attention and be concerned with what others think. If you've ever spent time around kids, you know that as toddlers, they all start to understand that specific behaviors can draw attention to them.

This attention-seeking becomes a habit that we carry into adulthood in various ways.

Some children realize that if they act ill, adults will be kind and take care of them. Later in life, these individuals are likely to exhibit hypochondriacal behaviours.

In the same vain, many children realize that achievement gets them showered with praise. Later in life, such individuals could become overachievers.

This shows that our actions are often predicated on how others will respond, whether or not we are aware.

The fact that young girls are frequently indoctrinated to believe that their value is purely dependent on whether they'll make a good wife or mother fuels our already troubling drive for attention and people pleasing.

Women are, as a result, adopting habits that are oriented on appeasing others rather than on accomplishing our own goals.

Boys are brought up to go for their dreams, whereas girls are brought up to go after what they think is expected of them.

In order to overcome these ingrained obstacles that prevent you from being your authentic self, you must stop putting so much emphasis on pleasing other people.

Recognize that it's acceptable if one woman's dream is radically dissimilar from yours, and quit making excuses for refusing to go after your dream.

It's very okay to be different (unique) from other women and more so, to start being goal-oriented for yourself.

For years, many women lead double lives as devoted wife and mom, lifestyle coaches or yoga instructors. The other half of that life is the reality behind that blog or that yoga studio, which involves working 60-hour to 80-hour weeks doing other things and micromanaging things in order to avoid having their lives fall apart.

This double life is due to the fact that, like many other working women, they are keenly aware that after a major change– marriage, childbirth, a lot of people are expecting them to reduce their work hours.

After all, popular opinion states that someone working as much as they are could never devote the appropriate amount of time needed to be a good mom.

This is why one of the biggest excuses for not following your dream is telling yourself, well, that's not what other women do.

One of the issues is that most people do nor want to stand out during their adolescence.

Of course, there are those rebels who try to stand out by being very outspoken and wearing loud outfits, but many more are too concerned with what others think, and they find comfort in being just like every other girl.

As a result, years of conformity can go unnoticed before you ask yourself, "Does being like every other woman really make me satisfied and fulfilled?"

Then, when you consider pursuing the aspirations that would bring you satisfaction and fulfillment, you may feel guilt for desiring something other women appear not to want.

The truth is, you shouldn't let others determine your self-worth or make you feel guilty for pursuing what you want out of life. Some women are happiest when they're looking after their home, and that is great, but you shouldn't apologize if that's not you.

CHAPTER 1: EXCUSES TO DROP

We women tend to give excuses to explain why we are not following our dreams.

These excuses are usually self-proclaimed and we repeat them to ourselves until they become a mantra that when someone asks, like reflex, they're out there.

To be successful, we need to drop these excuses like hot potatoes. All they do is hinder us from going after growth in whatever capacity we choose, and we're not having that.

EXCUSE 1: I'M NOT A GOAL-ORIENTED PERSON

A common reason for giving up on our dreams before we even start is saying, we're not a goal-oriented person.

Of course, it takes more than sitting on our derriere and hoping we would somehow achieve our goals, but here's the good news: goal-setting is a skill just like any other which can be learnt.
You can become more organized and productive.

We can create time for our goals and overcome insecurities through personal growth.

EXCUSE 2: I DON'T HAVE TIME.

We've all dismissed an exciting new idea with the excuse, "Sounds awesome, but I don't have the time."

Now, girl, this is just another excuse that must be sacked from your head.

It's a phrase that we all use quite often, but we should learn to eliminate it from our vocabulary.

To follow your dreams, you must make time for them.

Stop asking for free time to work on those goals and start making it happen.

You will undoubtedly make sacrifices, but you'll soon be reaping the benefits of your efforts.

The first step towards making time is to accept responsibility for your life.

Whether you're a stay-at-home mum or a CEO, you must accept responsibility for your time and schedule, including leisure activities like watching television.

After all, if busy moms and executives can find time to join yoga clubs, you can definitely find time for your goals too.

Remember that these unpleasant changes, such as giving up social media on weekdays will eventually pay off and bring you closer to fulfillment.

If you find it difficult to make time, try to create a schedule listing every hour of how you currently spend one week.

Then find a minimum of five hours anywhere within this week during which you will commit to actively pursuing that goal.

These hours don't have to be consecutive but must be at times when you're at your best – morning, afternoon or night.

Try out this new plan for the week ahead and, over the course of the week, imagine any changes you would like to make so the following week's plan is even better.

EXCUSE 3: IT'S ALREADY BEEN DONE.

Don't let "it's already been done" stop you from pursuing your goal. God knows it already gets in the way of many women.

"Why should I even bother if there are others already doing something similar?"

If you're good at making cute braids, you might see someone else advertising their saloon with a nice fan base, and then give up your potentially lucrative business without even giving it a chance.

What is happening here is that you're comparing your beginning against someone else's career, which is very wrong.

Look around you, a lot of success stories began with failed first attempts.

Most first tries are just a necessary stepping stone to greater things.

Remember, just because it's been done doesn't mean there's no one out there specifically searching for what you have.

KEYNOTE:

As kids, we all learned attention-seeking behaviors, and whether we like it or not, most of our actions now are made based on how those around us will respond.

These factors, along with the fact that many girls are still being raised to believe their value lies solely in how good they'll be as a mother and wife, stop many women from pursuing their dreams and feeling the need to apologize if they eventually do.

Have you ever heard this?
Boys are taught to follow their dreams, while girls are taught to follow what they believe is expected of them.

How can a woman get past this? Simple! Just stop worrying about other people's expectations.

Your dream does not have to look like or align with other's, and you shouldn't feel guilty for that.

Break all those excuses and begin to build behaviours that will catapult you to the top.

To achieve your goals, you must stop making excuses.

CHAPTER 2: ATTITUDES TO ADOPT

In the words of Historian Laurel Thatcher Ulrich, "Well-behaved women seldom make history."

When you think about that, you'd realize that it's alright to break social norms and fully embrace your ambition.

My first piece of advice is to stop asking for permission. You are the only authority you need to fight for your dreams.

STOP ASKING PERMISSION

Stop apologizing for everything.

Stop using too many pleasantries in an email or a sentence. Learn to cut them off. You won't appear as uncultured or untrained if you use other words in place of sorry.

'I apologize, but I would have to refuse' sounds way more assertive than, 'Please I'm sorry, but I cannot do this'.

"Sorry, please, excuse me, pardon me" No, cut them out.

Remove those adjectives and get to the point!

I understand this can be hard for some, but you come off as insecure and needy when your every sentence is saturated with please and sorry.

No, darling, we're not having that here.

Allow me to show you how this plays out in the workplace.

When an opportunity presents itself for someone to take on a new business initiative, women often ask for permission to pursue it, while men will immediately seize that opportunity.

While women are asking "pretty please", men are taking those projects and tasks that will give them both visibility and access to the decision-makers who are critical for their upward mobility.

This plays out in every rung of the corporate ladder.

Men don't ask for permission to speak up in meetings once they believe they have a valuable contribution to make. They are proactive and will find a way to make their voices heard.

Many women, however, will sit back and wait to be called on for a contribution or tentatively make a suggestion lacking conviction.

Imagine this; A male colleague claims a female colleague's idea as his own and gets away with it because the woman who brought the idea failed to 'own' it. If that idea was an important one, it could cause him to shoot up the corporate ladder, or get accolades for it.

This is obviously unfair, but we let this happen all the time and have no one to blame but ourselves.

We must create our own opportunities in business by taking the initiative rather than passively waiting and letting others dictate the course of our career trajectory.

If there is only one thing you take away from this book, it should be this: stop asking for permission to be successful. You are all the authority you need, and the only one whose permission is needed.

Business opportunities present themselves in the form of challenges that need to be solved, and we need to voluntarily and promptly run with these opportunities.

If you wait to ask for permission to pursue them, chances are, they will be long gone by the time the permission is given.

The era of sitting still and looking pretty is gone, sister.

TAKE CREDIT FOR YOUR WORK

Have you ever offered an idea in a meeting and gotten ignored, but then, seconds later, a man repeats the idea and everyone calls it brilliant? Have you ever worked your ass off on a team project and then got left off the thank-you email?

I know I have experienced these scenarios, and I'll tell you now, it isn't pleasant.

If we fail to be thoughtful about the manner in which we present our ideas at work, we risk not being heard or missing out on the credit we are due.

It's very important for us to be strategic with our suggestions and insights, because we get less credit when we work in groups with men, so as to avoid that infuriating feeling of being glazed over.

Getting credit for your work is not always easy.

You can do a great job, but if no one knows you were responsible for those results, you won't get recognized.

A way to get credit for your work is loudly promoting yourself and making sure people know exactly what it is you did.

This includes the work you've done, projects you worked on, and the sterling ideas you came up with.

If you fail to do this proactively, you're making it easy for others to intentionally or unintentionally steal credit for your work.

There are two types of people who take credit for others' work.

The first is the person who takes all the credit at the very last minute even though they did minimal work. Fact is, you were the one who did almost all of the work over a long period of time, but they manage to get credit by sweeping in at the eleventh hour.

Second is the person who takes more credit even when you both contributed equally to the task. This person is better at taking credit than you are. In some cases, because they're more popular than you are, others may give them the credit—and this person fails to share it with you.

People who steal credit create the perception that they did all the work. Keyword being 'perception'. The problem here is that perception becomes reality among decision-makers when it's not timely addressed.

A major reason people don't get credit for their work is that they choose to work behind the scenes and are reluctant to "toot their own horn."

This is a common practice in the competitive corporate world– our very own rat race.

To avoid getting your credit stolen, you have to get engaged in launching your own public relations campaign.

The following strategies will not only help you avoid this common problem but will also help increase your visibility in your organization. By expanding your influence and popularity, you'll be in a much less vulnerable position for credit theft.

Be proactive in exerting your influence.

There's a major difference between bragging and keeping others informed of your contributions.
People are often too passive when it comes to sharing their talents and accomplishments. This allows others to take credit due them.

To avoid this, be very active letting people know what exactly it is you contributed to a project, assignment or group discussion.

Place yourself as an authority/someone in the know.

To be able to openly share your knowledge with others, you need to trust in your knowledge.

No one else would believe what you are selling when you yourself do not believe in it.

Once people see this trust, they would respect and come to rely on your advice and input.

This involvement makes you a key contributor to the success of a project.

Let others know what you have done.

You must learn to tell others exactly what you have done or contributed.

Did you gather all the information to be refined?

Did you interview the study subjects?

Did you work on the graphs?

What exactly did you do?

If you feel like you would come off as bragging, just tell a story about how you faced a challenge and ultimately overcame it.

People love stories, and a nice story will stick in their brain and they will remember that fondly.

Make your contribution completely visible.

Find opportunities to present your ideas so others will appreciate what you know and what you have done.

Prepare ideas on topics before the meetings, so you'd be able to add more value on the spot.

Chime in when a colleague talks about a project that could benefit from your expertise.

This type of visibility directly shapes how others view you and your value to your organization.

Seek out projects you can own.

Find them and own them.

These projects can be big or small, but that's not important.

The goal here is to completely own them so your name would be on them, front and center.

Bold, if possible.

This makes it hard for anyone else to take your credit.

You're the person responsible, the woman in charge.

The responsibility might appear too great and scary that you get cold feet. Wrap those feet in wool socks and place them next to the fireplace, because you're taking that bull by the horn.

It might fail, but you know what else?
It might be a success.

Don't hide behind the scenes.

It may appear that working behind the scenes is the safest option because if a project fails, your name will not be associated with it.

However, you want to be at the front of the pack if you wish to truly excel.

Be the spokesperson.

Generally speaking, the person who presents a project to a group automatically receives credit. So, in order to counteract our cultural tendency to undervalue our contributions, women may want to ask male colleagues if they can be the ones to do the talking.

Tell them you want to do the talking, even.

While these steps can help us combat workplace discrimination, resolving this issue is the joint responsibility of everyone.

We all wish to believe in a better world; one where hard work pays off.

However, as long as women fail to receive full credit for their contributions, they'll remain stuck on the sidelines while men reap the benefits of collaborative success.

ASK FOR HELP

It can be uncomfortable to ask for help — as adults, we'd like to believe we're self-sufficient and capable of navigating whatever life throws at us on our own, but whether we need a bit of help, advice, or simply someone to talk to, we all need to rely on others from time to time, and there's no shame in doing so.

In fact, asking for help brings you closer to the people who are the most important.

Here are a few simple tips to boost your confidence in asking for help and getting the assistance you require.

<u>Understand that people want to help.</u>

We are constantly terrified that asking for help will make us appear inept.

That is not the case, as admitting that you cannot do everything is a sign of intelligence.

<u>Get rid of that widespread belief that no one is willing to help.</u>

What makes humans unique is our ability to help one another and pay it forward.

People feel good when they help others– it's nice to feel needed.

<u>Don't be afraid of rejection.</u>

Many women avoid asking for help because they are afraid of being told no, which may stem from a fear of rejection.

We avoid asking because being rejected is associated with pain and failure, so we avoid this pain by not asking.

Just because someone says no does not always imply that they are rejecting you.

<u>Just Ask.</u>

And if you don't ask, you'll never know if you would have gotten what you asked for.

Why suffer in silence when you can seek assistance?

CHAPTER 3: SKILLS TO ACQUIRE

With your foundation of empowering behaviors, there are certain skills that can help you reach your goals.

As with any skill, these are things you can get better at with some intentional practice.

These are really helpful skills you need to acquire for sustained success.

PLANNING

If you believe that you're terrible at planning, try this road map exercise: set your goal at the finish line, then work backward.

Think about what needs to happen in order for you to get to the finish line from your current position.

Brainstorm as many useful ideas as you can think of, then narrow down to three most important and smaller goals which will get you to your main target.

For example, you might decide to publish a book.

Though you may have all sorts of research and publication ideas, three important bite-sized goals would be to make a book proposal, hire a literary agent and submit the proposal to publishers.

It is important to be specific with your goals.

Rather than putting "write your book" on your to-do list, tell yourself to "write a thousand words." You'll find this to be a much more effective approach.

CONFIDENCE

The next skill is confidence.

To paint a picture of the gender disparity when it comes to confidence, a recent study showed that men will often apply for a job if they feel they meet 60 percent of the role's criteria, while women tend to only apply if they're 100 percent qualified.

Girl, go for that interview. Don't forget that you can grow on the job, even if it's a challenging one.

Think of one time you threw caution to the wind and went for something even when you felt you were not qualified.

Did you get it? What did the experience teach you?

Did you get rejected?

What did that teach you?

At least you tried, and trying has never killed anyone. Remember, the worst you could get is a 'no'.

When you think about it, you would see that doubt is the root of it all.

How many times have you spotted something wrong and refused to speak about it then someone else points it out later?

The point, however, is not to be right the entire time, but to be able to speak out cohesively and assertively about a matter, asking intelligent questions along the way.

Start with Small Risks and Work Your Way Up

There have been several studies which find that women are generally more risk averse than men and while I'm not entirely convinced, I have found that starting with small risks and them paying off boosts my confidence with larger ones.

It is the same for you, right?

For example, you realize that you ask for permission for a lot of things at work, which clearly isn't very good for a leader.

You can simply start with something not too big and just do it, then iterate.

These things are hard in practice, but the saying 'practice makes perfect' is there for a reason.

Needless to say, many women find the cost of taking up space, or the fear of earning it, prohibitively expensive, and prefer invisibility instead.

The thought we have is, 'If I stay invisible, maybe I'll be safe.' Perhaps I can avoid the trolling, personal attacks, casual dismissals, double standards, and the agony of being rejected and objectified before I can even be heard.'

Is it any surprise that so many women decide to make excuses for their brilliance and hide their true ability, sometimes even from themselves, if this is the price of occupying spaces of greatness?

Confidence says, go for it! Doesn't matter, break a wing, break a leg, just do it.

You'll see it was worth it to take up your space in the room when your name elicits respect.

Take up space by saying your ideas, speaking up when you feel your rights are being trampled on, walking with your head held high, and refusing to step down for someone else on the sole basis that that someone is a 'he'.

Finally, leadership may not come naturally but you can definitely learn it.

When you think of "leaders", you may see a person in a power suit sitting in an intimidating office, but that is not the reality.

You are also a leader.

You can change the world and make it brighter by letting the fire inside you glow for everyone to see.

PERSISTENCE

Dream big, start small.

Of course, it is important to have a vision and plan your way into achieving it as this will give you a sense of direction, but don't get too lost in trying to tackle all your goals at once.

Yes, we must dream big, but remember, we won't get anywhere if we don't start with the least amount of work possible.

Getting up in the morning is a start.

Opening our book to the first page is another.

Apart from avoiding us getting overwhelmed, doing small tasks can get us through the day.

It's easy to get burnt out when we keep working without seeing the light at the end of the tunnel. The trick to this is to light a little fire and take it one step at a time.

To avoid giving up and getting burnt out, we have to determine when something is no longer working.

Note that this doesn't mean we've made the wrong decision, but that there must be another way to go about it.

In this part of the process, we must become creative. It could be that the right tools are not available, hence the need to craft them ourselves. It could also be that we need to forge our own path for something that has never been done before.

Doing the same things repeatedly without seeing results can hinder our persistence. If we find new solutions, no matter how little, this can help ignite a newfound energy that will keep us going.

Know the reason behind your goals to be persistent.

The secret to doing more is having a source of motivation, and this motivation lies in the reasons we do the things we do.

Because reasons reap results, to persist is to keep coming back to the "whys" and letting them fuel us to keep going.

LEAD-(H)ER-SHIP

Previous advice has stated that to be successful in the workplace, you need to keep your head down and put in the work. This works in the faith that over time, you'll be noticed and your work recognized.

Apparently, you just need to grind things out for a year or two.

Let's be honest here. We know that's not the reality. If we choose to follow that advice, we'd spend decades waiting for recognition that's not coming by itself.

Darling, you own your career. Step outside the day-to-day activities and build relationships and connections across your organization.

Take mentorship seriously.

Find sponsors and feel free to have meaningful conversations with senior-level individuals. They don't bite.

When opportunities arise, you would be top of mind, because not only have you been putting in the work, but you've been letting everyone know what you can do and what you want to do.

As a leader, you get to decide the shape and distance of your lane.

Veto as you wish, and keep negative people away from you– it's your space.

See yourself as an entrepreneur even within your office.

NEGOTIATING AS A LEAD(H)ER

Corporate management has, intentionally or not, created an atmosphere of fear around negotiating anything from salary to resources.

As a lead(h)er, rather than putting forward an ask and waiting with bated breath to see if you're rejected, you can change your mindset into thinking of negotiations as opportunities for win-win outcomes.

They're not doing you any favours as they benefit from you being there and the services you render.

Say, you work in a laboratory and you want an electron microscope because you feel your work will be twice as fast with it than with the simple microscope you already have, you wouldn't go with the 'Please and pretty please', but with confidence.

Find out what makes your request an easy "yes" from the management.

Have the mindset of you being two companies working out a business deal.

Put out your terms and conditions, listen to them bring theirs and settle on a win-win situation.

Next, think about your best alternative to the negotiated agreement.

If your request was noted and the company states that there is not enough funds for an electron microscope as they are working on a different project, you should try to close the gap between what was offered and what you want.

They may offer a compound microscope instead, considering it fits their budget and you could offer to wait for the duration of, say, six months to let them settle their other project and get their money.

They know you need it badly, and you can remind them of the agreement after six months.

This way, you get what you want and they don't stretch themselves thin trying to satisfy everyone.

This could even go to show how reasonable you are. Way better than throwing a tantrum and claiming you wouldn't get anything done without it ASAP.

These conversations can be hard to have and need practice, so you find a balance between reasonable requests and demanding for impossible things.

This is why it is very important to build negotiation skills.

You would need to leverage your mentors, rely on your network, gain feedback on how you should approach the conversation and set the groundwork with the impact you've been having.

You cannot have this impact without everything we have gone through in this book: the habits to drop, taking credit for your work, networking, asking for help (increases your likeability), being confident and being persistent.

Don't let others decide how your career will go— it's yours for a reason.

Build your network, be proactive in showing your worth, and learn to negotiate like a boss.

You're the leader you should admire.

CONCLUSION

DARLING, BELIEVE IN YOUR DANG SELF!

Believing in yourself means having faith in your own capabilities.

It means believing you can do what you set out to do, even when it looks really tough.

When you believe in yourself, you'd overcome self-doubt and have the confidence to take action and get things done. Only when you believe in yourself, as confidence is a direct result of self-trust.

When you're drowning in fears, and self-sabotaging behaviors (like we mentioned earlier), success falls out of your grasp.

All the books, training, and motivational speeches in the world won't change your life.

When you struggle with confidence, you tend to focus only on things you can't do. This is because you feel weaknesses more keenly, highlight them in your mind and soon cannot see any other thing.

"I'm bad at this," quickly becomes, "I'm bad at everything!"

Darling, everyone has weaknesses. The same way everyone has strengths.

You have badass strengths.

You must identify your strengths, to get the most benefits from them.

Here are a few tips to start building confidence now. Apply them in every aspect of your life, deliberately, and see the magic happen.

This girl still believes in magick.

Stop spinning your wheels at things you aren't wired for.

Find what you are already good at, and work at becoming great at that.

A common habit of successful people is to focus on their strengths, what they excel at and enjoy, then delegate weaknesses to others rather than worry about not measuring up.

When you shift your focus to developing your strengths, you'll effortlessly feel more competent and confident.

How can you have faith in yourself when you don't even know who you really are? Or worse, when you are trying hard to be someone you're not.

This is the next tip.

Know yourself.

We've all been there at some point in our lives– trying to please others by hiding our true self, or just trying to fit in and camouflaging.

Self-confidence comes from embracing who you are and what's important to you– this varies greatly with individuals. Self-confidence does not arise from being inauthentic or trying to please others.

Life most life hacks, this is easier said than done.

The pressure to 'fit in' is strong, and starts from a very young age. This is okay if your goal is to have an unremarkable life.

The fact that you've reached so far in this book however, tells a different story. You want something more.

To start believing you can have that life you've always wanted, you must understand the things that make you unique, and celebrate those things. They're all you and to find them, you would have to dig deep.

What truly makes you you? What are your true values? What kind of human is beneath all the social tags?

When you live life true to your identity and core values, you will begin to believe in your worth, abilities, and potential.

Your core values are the building blocks for forming your own philosophy to guide your actions moving forward.

Embracing yourself is best done in baby steps, because most times, we've been conditioned to hate who we truly are. We see our core values as being too weird, too weak, or too lackluster.

Darling, from now onwards, we're not living life on the terms of anyone but ourselves.

Start your journey to self-realization by writing down what's important to you.

Try to do this several times over weeks and months. You'll see that each time, you get closer to uncovering your core values.

This will help you see through those things you've been conditioned to believe in and when you're finished, you'll have a list of traits that represent 'you' in the purest form.

Most women feel the need to apologize for their ambitions when they don't fit into the traditional roles women are told to be happy settling for.

This should stop, darling, because women should never apologize for having their own dreams and goals in life, and they should never ask for permission to chase those dreams.

The behaviors I highlighted earlier can help women achieve their goals, such as learning to ask for help and building a solid foundation for success by taking credit for their work amongst others.
Acquiring skills like planning, persistence and confidence goes a long way too.

Lastly, remember that if you fail to believe in yourself, no one else will. When you believe you can do it, chances are more times than not, you actually can!

Darling, apologizing is so last season.

www.ingramcontent.com/pod-product-compliance
Lightning Source LLC
Chambersburg PA
CBHW071124240526
45465CB00023B/808